This book belongs to
a very good swimmer.

Use your thumb print to make your mark.

I dedicate this book to anyone who has ever felt like they weren't enough.
You are enough. You always were.
You always will be. - Chris

For all the young ones out there who see the world through
a kaleidoscopic lens, I see you.
Thanks to my sister, LauraMichel, for always seeing me. - Ariel

Edited by V. Ruiz and Winona Mann

Published by Wheat Penny Press, an imprint of Row House Publishing
ISBN 9798986827346 Hardcover
ISBN 9798986827353 eBook
Printed in China
Distributed by Simon & Schuster

Library of Congress Cataloging in Publication data available upon request

Fonts used in the design of this book Vanilla Twilight and Comic Sans.
The artwork was created by hand in Procreate and Photoshop.

First Edition
10  9  8  7  6  5  4  3  2  1

# YOU'RE A GOOD SWIMMER

Words by Christopher Rivas
Art by Ariel Boroff

You're a good swimmer.

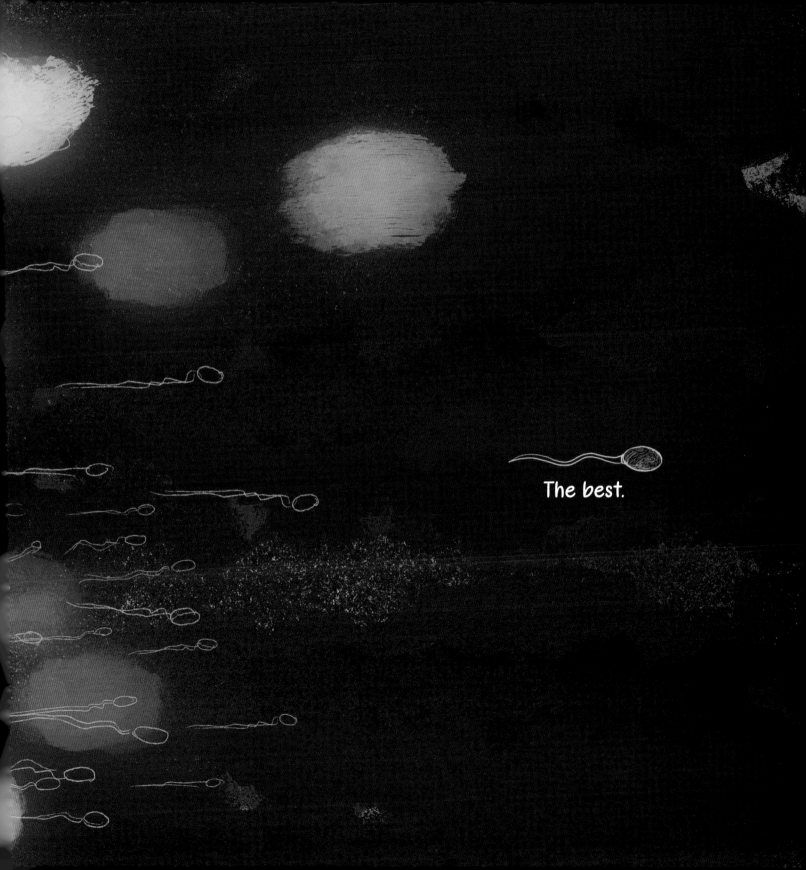

The best.

A champion.

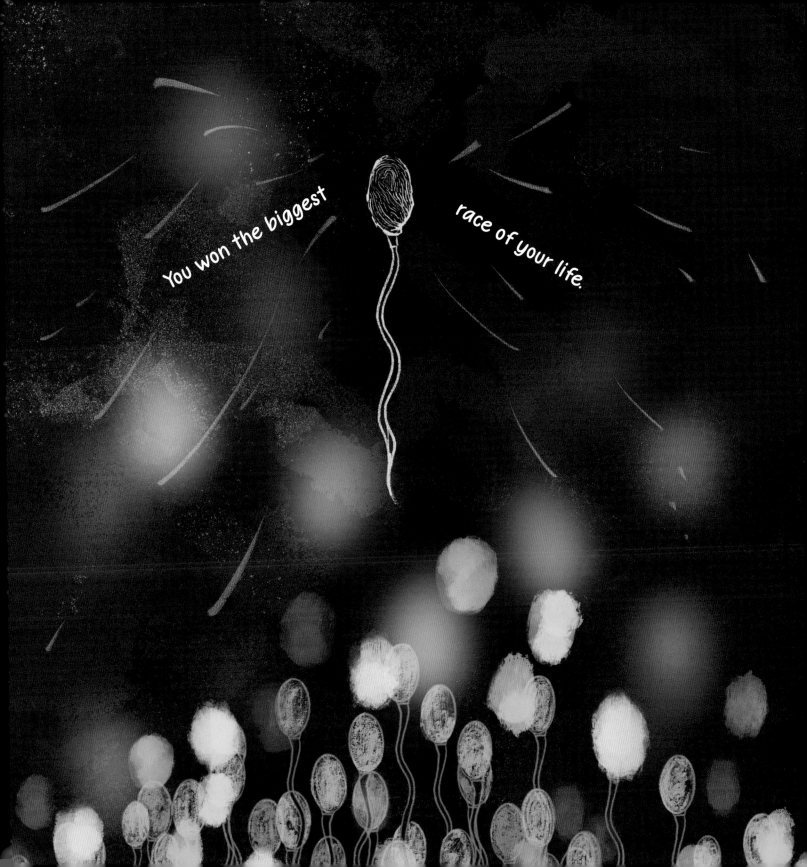

You might not remember, but it's true.

You and every living being represent a cosmic victory.

Imagine: you versus MILLIONS.

The winner gets the prize we call life.

You are that winner.
You won. You made this happen.

You swam fast. You swam hard.

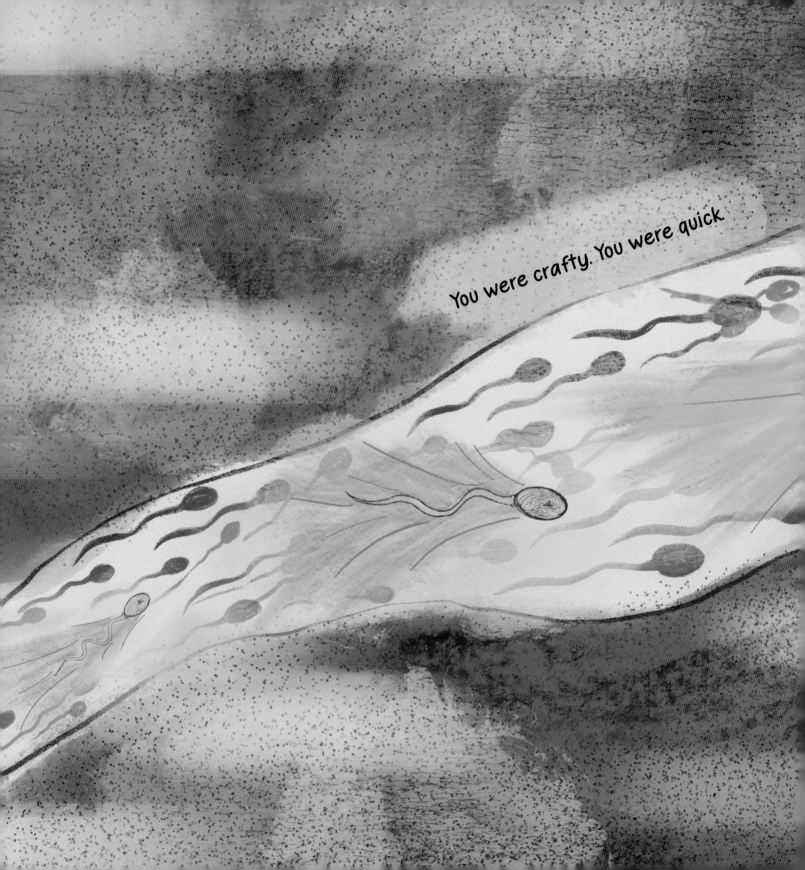

You were smart and a little wild.

You refused to give up, even when the numbers were against you.

Even when it felt overwhelming. Even when the race got hard and you thought you had no chance. You persevered.

Then, an organ called the placenta nourished and protected you,
and helped you grow.

Something mysterious, immense, and profound had already decided,
since the beginning of time, that you would exist.

It was the most important race of your life, and all the forces of
the universe cooperated so that you could be here.

Because your presence was desired in this WORLD.

Not to mention all of the things that had to go exactly as they did for a particular set of people to be able to dance with each other long enough for you to get to the starting line.

START

They danced because you are needed. Here. NOW.

You are the product of a complex web of ancestors, wisdom, and perfect timing, spiraling back for billions of years. Each of your ancestors grew wise and strong and gave breath to a descendant, who gave breath to another descendant, who gave breath to you.

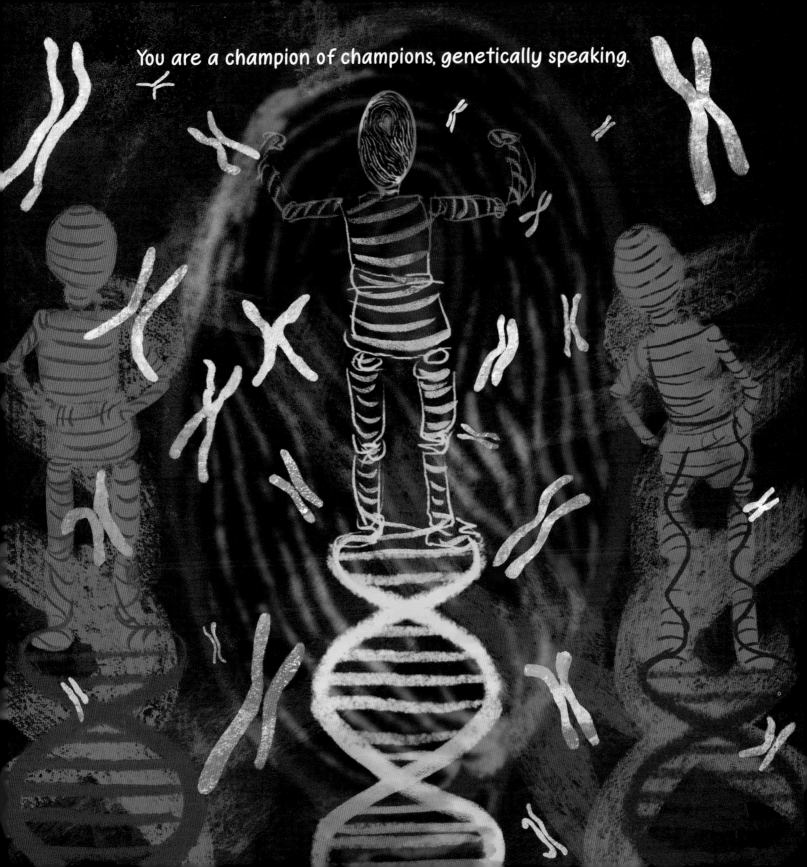

We are so grateful that you won.
We are so grateful that you were born a winner.

YOU are here.

And if you ever forget, remember that you are exactly where you need to be.

Even when life feels hard, even in the ups and downs,
you are always growing and learning.

You grew and grew and grew from a single cell formed by the union of a sperm and an egg. They divided into two, then four, then eight, and so on to become the trillions of cells that are you.

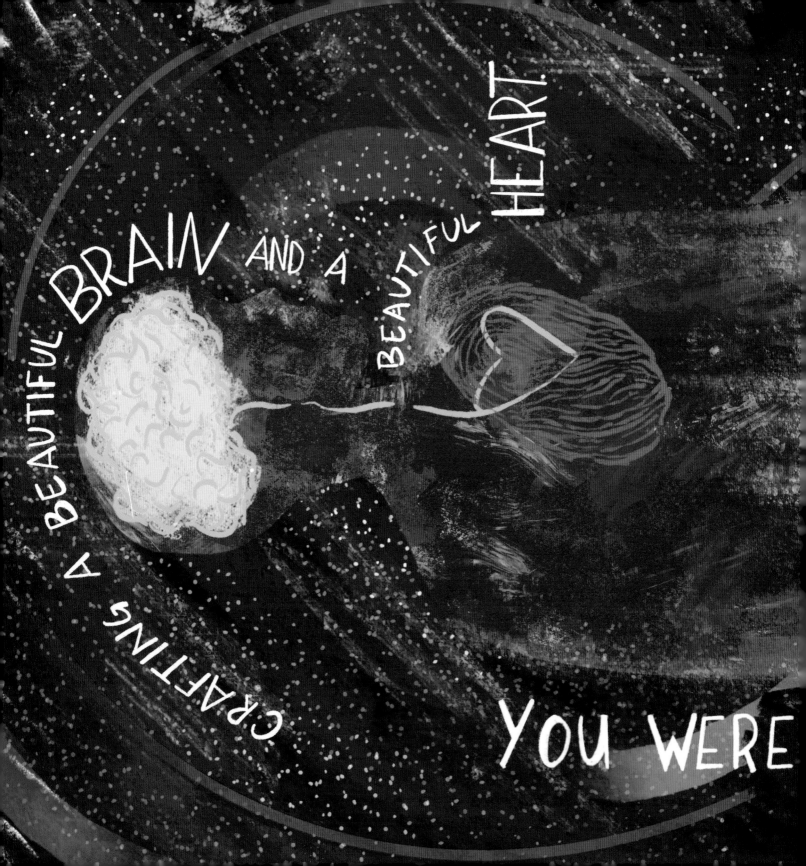

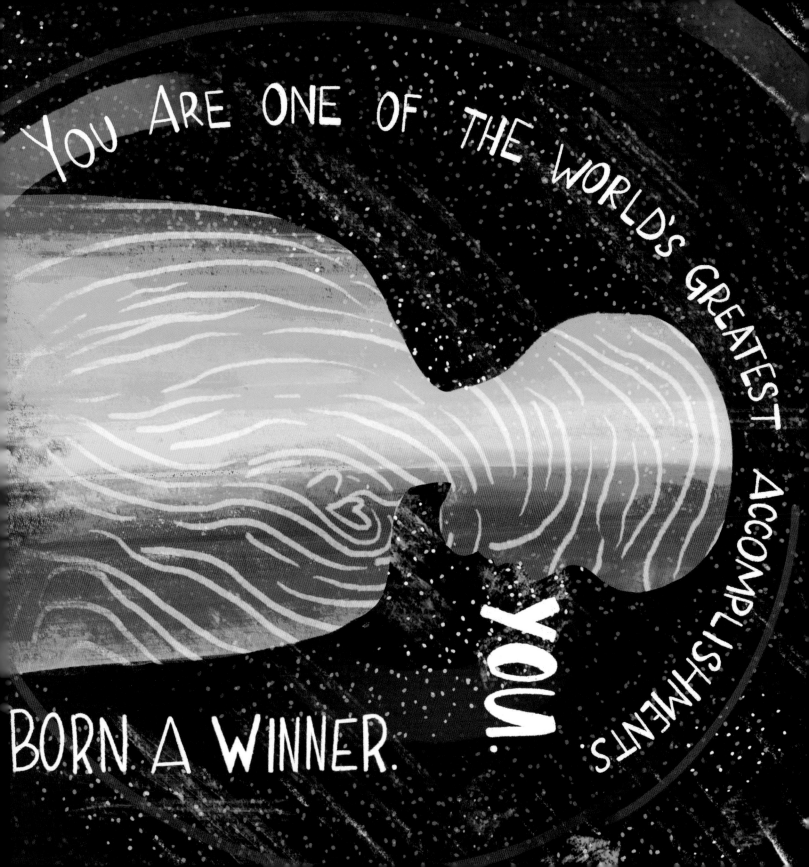

# GLOSSARY

**Ancestor** — Someone from your family who lived a long time ago, like your great grandparents or even older relatives. They are the people who came before you in your family.

**Descendant** — A person who comes after you in your family, like your children, grandchildren, or even great grandchildren. They are the family members who are born later and are part of future generations.

**DNA** — DNA is a special code inside your body that carries instructions for how you look and how your body works. It's part of what makes you uniquely you.

**Egg cell or Ovum** — An egg cell, also known as an ovum, is the largest cell in the human body and the only human cell you can see without a microscope. When it is fertilized by a sperm cell, it can develop into a **zygote**, and eventually, an **embryo**. Egg cells are huge, about as wide as a strand of hair! That may sound small, but no other cell comes close to being that large.

**Embryo** — An embryo is the next step after a **zygote**. When sperm cells and **egg** cells from grown ups come together, they make a zygote. This zygote then grows and changes into an embryo, marking the next exciting stage in the baby-making journey!

**Evolution** — Evolution is how living things change slowly over a very, very long time. It's where plants and animals learn to adapt and become different to survive and thrive in their homes.

**Fallopian tubes** — Fallopian tubes are tiny pathways in a person's body that carry the **zygote** to the uterus. This journey through a fallopian tube is an important step in growing a baby.

**Fertilization** — Fertilization is the process where a **sperm** cell joins with an **egg** cell, combining their **genetic** material. It's the important first step in the creation of new life in plants, animals, and humans.

**Genes and Chromosomes** — A gene is like a page in a book called a chromosome. This book is inside every cell of your body and holds all the important information that makes you who you are. Genes and chromosomes decide things like the color of your eyes, how tall you might grow, what color your hair will be, and even if you think cilantro tastes yummy or like soap. Most people have about twenty-five thousand genes and twenty-three chromosomes.

**Gene pool** — A gene pool is a big collection of different genes, the instructions that living things share. It's a mix of all the traits that make each plant, animal, and person different and interesting.

# GLOSSARY

**IVF** — In Vitro Fertilization (IVF), is a way some families make a baby. It's like a helping hand in a lab that brings together sperm cells and egg cells from two grown ups to start the process of reproduction.

**Ovaries** — Ovaries are a place inside the human body where eggs are kept. About once a month, an egg is released from one of two ovaries. If a sperm cell fertilizes the egg cell, together they become a zygote.

**Placenta** — The placenta is a temporary organ that grows inside the uterus during pregnancy. The placenta gives the growing baby all the food and protection they need, making sure they're safe and sound until they're ready to meet the world.

**Reproduction** — Reproduction is how living things make more of themselves. It's nature's way of creating new plants, animals, and people to keep the world full of life and diversity.

**Sperm** — Sperm cells are microscopic reproductive cells—little swimmers—responsible for fertilizing the egg during reproduction. Even though they're tiny, sperm cells are really fast! When one lucky sperm cell reaches the egg cell first, they team up to start making a new person.

**Uterus** — The uterus, also called the womb, is a pear-shaped organ that's like a cozy space inside a grown-up's tummy. It's where the baby can grow and be safe. The uterus is a warm, snug home for little ones before they are born.

Zinc spark — A zinc spark looks like a tiny, sparkly fireworks show that happens when a **sperm** cell **fertilizes** an **egg** cell. This burst of sparkles is made of something called zinc. Ask your grown-up to help you search for "zinc sparks" online. They're very fun to watch.

Zygote — A zygote is a combination of cells that happens when the **egg** cell and **sperm** cell from different grown-ups come together. This mix of cells is full of the instructions needed to start growing a unique baby. After about four days, a zygote will grow into an **embryo**.